A
Personality Syndrome II

BriGeor

[bree-jour]

THIS IS FOR BROTHER DAVID.

I GIVE MY THANKS OF APPRECIATION

FOR YOUR ENCOURAGEMENT MANY YEARS AGO.

AND

TO THE MEN WHO HAVE GIVEN ME MY PEN NAME
ALONG WITH A HEART FULL OF LOVE.

CONTENTS

The BriGeor Philosophy

"If you've been there,

You don't have to explain it.

If you haven't,

You can't".

Introduction

In writing The Original Personality Syndrome, I gave names to

different kinds and types of personalities. [However, it will be published later for

your pleasure!] Have you heard someone describe a person – and

the reply is – yes, I know the type! You may not know the individual but

you know the personality. There are variations from which we build

individual personalities. There are hundreds of thousands personalities

that you will recognize. You won't find them all here . . . very similar to the

many millions of people that exist. The combinations are endless. There

are similar with endless combinations. Not enough time and space to

record them all. Here are enough ideas to combine that will get the ole

thinking cap buzzing. Smile every now and then. It's good for you.

It was my desire to point out and help maybe one or two million people

become aware. As I have stated and named in another book,

Unawareness Disease is quite rampant and running faster than we can

seem to catch up. There are those who think that we arrive in this life and

unfortunately are unaware that we need to keep growing because

it never will be a reason good enough to stop learning and growing. Was it

Albert who stated that we do the same thing over and over again and

expect a different outcome each time? Believe me – I know – and how

you might inquire? Ha! Figure that one out . . . nah; several of us have done it a time or two. Don't raise your hand – it's a private thing. Plus, you don't have to show everyone you had an unacceptable action at one time because it isn't good to dwell on it. Don't you know that at one time they have seen it? So the Unawareness Disease doesn't bite you, just be aware. So, as I name [once again although different] some of these syndromes, feel free to laugh! It is when we laugh at ourselves that we let go and grow. Move on – it will look so petty years from now if we hang on to the hurts, snarls and snares that keep us down.

You have seen bitter men and women who are separated, divorced, or just plain single who have been hurt at one time or another. It is their life's mission to continue throughout this life with any hurts they once had or thought they had and remain a bitter ole crow for the remainder. Oh, and by the way – let them fester, grow and feed them some more. Wow and you thought the "I'm a victim role" was gone with the golden days of past. Please!

When touchy problems come along – and you don't have a non-biased party to see clearly for you; then remember that you have read that you don't have to accept it – keep it or embrace it. It's not yours, so pass it on down the drain or let it go with the wind. Don't catch or keep that which you don't want to embrace. Only you can make the decision to claim or toss. As the age old mystery goes – some will and some won't. Some know how to let go and some don't. Some want to grow and some don't see the need for enlightenment. So, if you find light, soak it up and maybe some of it will shine on others who need it. Actions do speak louder than words any day.

If you by chance recognize a trait seen in someone . . . fear not. I am not picking on anyone one in particular. I am shining the light on all of us. We all have room for improvement even if we don't see it. The point is to learn, and keep learning. Many times people have asked me when I am going to reach a point, get my degree and stop this nonsense. Oh, never! If I want to keep learning the mysteries of personalities – others and my own – there is no end to the growth and distance to become and achieve more – not in this life. May be one of the reasons why God in His infinite wisdom offers us eternity.

Mother has said many times that if people knew better, they would do better. Sounds like a rather simplistic statement at first. I certainly didn't give merit due to lack of ignorance. As time has flown by and this enlightenment comes to mind [It has, many times.] with much delight. She was and is right on the mark. She was way beyond my thinking. Now that she has been gone for over a decade, this statement echoes back the meaning stronger and deeper. She was a reader who never gave up the desire or need to learn.

There are some statements that my father made throughout the years that all of his children took for granted. He was beyond my thinking as well. [They made a great parenting team.] He saw things as they are and not how he wished they were. He persevered and never gave up hope for the prize. He usually got it. He read all the time and never gave up on learning and absorbing knowledge.

Learning is a grand thing to do. Using the things and ideas we learn for good is even better! As my dad once said of having a college degree, '" It's a tool. You need to have some common sense to go along with it. It's not any good to have it and then not use it."' My, how I loved those parents!

If anyone should have coined the idea of Unawareness Disease, it was my mother and father. They were gifted with the sight to see when others couldn't. They tried to share when others would not listen. They learned to share and then move on . . . with the hopes that one day their sharing would benefit someone.

In creating the BriGeor Collection, what a dream come true to be a part of the fruition of their love, caring, and sharing. Each time I write, it is with much pleasure if only one person's life is lifted. If one person can benefit from these thoughts, then it is only an extension of a loving man and woman who gave all they had to lift others up lovingly, to reach a potential of being the best, and enjoy the gifts and talents given to each of us. Don't forget that we turn this nurturing into our own style and creativity.

As you proceed in the following pages, know that you may see something that someone else may not see. Someone else may see something that you do not. Isn't it fun knowing that the same words in the same book is seen differently as different eyes glance upon the combinations that make up the personality syndromes that we are.

The following syndromes can be found anywhere and in any socioeconomic group. The common denominator found across the board is the age old idea of being human. It is good to invent new creative gadgets that can improve our day to day living. There are some great things that only a privileged few will enjoy. A key word to remember is things. Ideas are great when used for improvement, growth and lifting. Things are fun to have – in the end, it will be the ideas implemented to love that will matter and live generation to generation.

Using our minds and hearts to offer the timeless gifts of love is the one that lingers through the good and weathers the not so good times.

A

Personality Syndrome

II

A Personality Syndrome II

Named Syndromes are underlined.

1. <u>Mad Catch:</u> Being furious for being caught for doing something that shouldn't have been done.

2. <u>Unawareness Disease:</u> This particular syndrome will strangle, bite, starve and destroy you without feelings of total destructive behavior. This has danger written all over it. Examples appear later.

3. <u>You owe me:</u> This covers a broad spectrum of the rainbow. Small favor, feel good favors, helpful favors and pay back favors. This one can be dangerous for the person receiving the favor. Pay back can be somewhat of a pickle sometimes and costly.

4. <u>Better is mine:</u> Whether house, car, clothes, jewelry, things and more — it's just better than yours.

5. <u>Sloppy worker pay more:</u> This person smiles at you so sweetly; the voice will melt like sugar oozed from the South straight from the sugar cane. This sugary sweet thang will urgently need your help to make some extra cash in return for painting one or two rooms. As it turns out, the time turns into weeks instead of days. The bill turns into eyeball popping quadruple jaw dropping unbelievable gahoona nerve amount! The work performed? Let's just tell it like it is; messy, unfinished, uneven, and unacceptable!

Watch out for this dangerous one! You'll be charmed
by the sugar and poisoned by the touch!

6. <u>You Have More you owe me:</u> This one is tricky as well. The
    approach Is so pitiful, so sad, and so in need of your help.
    But come pay up time, well for sure you have more
    therefore you can afford it. Don't expect any repayment
    from me darling. You have more so you won't miss it. Look
    how much you have and I don't . . . even if you didn't gamble
    it, dope, or poop it away like me. Don't you remember when
    I did this for you or yours? Don't you know how much my
    advice is worth? Don't you realize how valuable I have been
    to you? Of course you owe me.

7. <u>Twist It, Shake It, and Work It:</u> Advice to a minor – no matter
    the age or stage, is unacceptable! Of course if this is the
    syndrome that's giving advice to a child, you got to wonder
    what kind of parent would do that. Would a caring, decent
    parent exude the character and ethics telling their child to
    twist it, shake it, and work it?

8. <u>Direct A Lot</u>: Also known as the micromanager; asks you to
    do something, but you have to hold your hand the way the
    "director" does, otherwise it is wrong. No regard for age or
    ability. Low EQ.

9. <u>Bet-A-Lew</u>: False security that illuminates a raw interior.
    Feels rather inferior to most except those that can be
    controlled by a bully/intimidating nature.

10. <u>Ugg-A-Lee Sneaker</u>: Smiling individual that has a conniving mind that continually clicks for a way to hurt someone and very inferior.

11. <u>Finer-roo</u>: Takes a while to understand this one and you never really do. Must admire the attitude is quite smart witted and fun to be around.

12. <u>Forget-A-Lot</u>: Nothing intentional, just doesn't remember, especially if you are not important enough to remember what is said or done. This one can be nice or naughty . . . depending upon the color of the heart. Do understand there is the intentional and unintentional one.

13. <u>Muse-Me</u>: Laughs a lot in conversations with a pseudo laughter that indicates insecurity. This is obvious to the observer, oblivious to the owner.

14. <u>Muffin Top</u>: A sweet individual, that is difficult to be around especially when doing something simple and easy. Does not know how to mingle into a group, does better with one on one. Needy individual, who, God bless 'em, just needs our patience and prayers.

15. <u>Baby-El</u>: Big hefty person that introduces self as the baby Sibling supposedly grown-up but sadly the body has gone into starvation mode to store fat to build a snowman with the stunted mind of a late blooming teen.

16. <u>Nanlew</u>: Likes to correct someone in public, not realizing that it makes them look like an idiot.

17. Jay-Lew-Nan: Remembers that a plan with a "friend" did not work out thirty some years earlier and is bitter toward the spouse for not returning upon command after throwing 'em out.

18. Nanja: Ugly physically, ugly inside and utterly ugly. Enough said.

19. Lewnan: Will do ANYTHING to hurt someone in any way shape or form. This one pretends to be smarter although inferior and quite may not see it.

20. Pignose: Looks like mama, acts like mama, and talks like mama. Hasn't grown emotionally or mentally to match the age. Does not have a clue as to their true looks. This is so sad.

21. Coke Harlot: Doped up, put out, and dumb down. Also known as rode hard, put up wet and dried out.

22. I Smarrt as You: Tells you they are as smart as you with your fancy college d-gree. After sincere thought, nah, couldn't get a teaching position like me, so, no, you're not as smart as me. Maybe in streets you have an advantage with crooked thinking. Smarter than me, I think not.

23. Stegaah: Feels superior, looks inferior. Tries to be and just isn't.

24. <u>Dusteve:</u> Walks up to you at an event with an arrogant attitude greeting and doesn't realize that he can be transparent, unequal, and unknowledgeable of things that were and things to come.

25. <u>Shicgoo:</u> Reprimands, demands and commands the situation if allowed to by any or all individuals near. Any response of rebuke is cause for put up, shut up and cut up.

26. <u>Meefee:</u> Can do or say what they feel, no matter that it steps on another individual. Now, should the tables be turned, you had better not do the same, otherwise you are in for a verbal whip lashing of threats.

27. <u>Ebb-Tider</u>: A person who doesn't really know you, threatens you if you repeat words shared. Tide in, Tide out and tied up.

28. <u>Silent Taker</u>: Why not just take what you are owed. After all, a gift of gab, bounty of flab, love of self and stuck on the shelf kind of person who feels you have more therefore, you owe more. Owed and blown up with importance should consider collecting from all the ones stroked along the way. Don't just pick all the goodies from one person.

29. <u>Miss-A-Priss</u>: Is the spouse of a self-proclaimed preacher that smiles like a chubby little cherry apple. She's so helpful, so sincere, and so deceptive. This one is very dangerous. Will legally lie and approve of family lovers. Dah, I am so smart and can fart kind of person, yet, so goodly, so goodie, and so gooey. Will throw up on you in a second and smile a sweet apple smile. Aren't I so precious?

30. Mackenclaw: Oh, so sweet and sugary. So full of slut and muck, it's hard to tell who she'll do next kind of person.

31. Clawcar: Stops by the church on pretense visit. Look closer and you'll see a sneaky touchy-touchy now and then. Gives new meaning to observe by the unseen one. Shine on the dark side is shown to be what it is. Ah, sweet touch a much for such a meet.

32. Wild-Eyed-Willie: A young person of unexposed existence who is offered a thoughtful gift with no thank you. Just a grab and stare . . . well, is that all?

33. Stale-A-Non: Stuck in time with no reason or rhyme. Fault of her own and fall of the dawn. No taste, no talent, and no tell.

34. Taste-A-Not: Judges all and too good for any. Sad to say, the eighties took plenty. Compassion is not visional - a few, who are afraid to look.

35. Think-knot-head: Soldier saying good bye to family preparing to deploy to the war zone. The loving friend tells the not as smart mother to get her passport updated 'cause she will need it if her son gets shot badly enough to be sent to Germany. What a lovely friend to be so thoughtful of a mother and her son. With implanting thoughts of this loving nature who needs enemies?

36. <u>Innocent—none gossiper-reaper mental case</u>: The husband makes an observation to his not so bright wife. She shares the information that her husband shared with her to the subject of the observation. It was a hurtful thing to share with the observed person in question. She must be mental to so bluntly state "her" facts. She's been sheltered. Poor thang; reaping havoc. Poor, poor, and poor thang. Could she be a mental case? Surely a sincere thoughtful person wouldn't be so cruel.

37. <u>In Styler-Not</u>: This particular individual thinks their looks are cool and suave. It's really sad . . . you can see the dumb oozing out the pores. It is difficult being around this one due to low life looks and exploding personalities when any disagreements arise.

38. <u>Goof da-love birds</u>: These cool lovers are so cool; they forgot to get unmarried before they got together. Ugh, didn't matter to them. Their feeling of superiority showed their lack of integrity. Oh, that's right; it's the in-slimy club to be a member for the under lifers. Yea, it fits.

39. <u>Monk-a-shoo, monk-a-shee, monk-a-shaa</u>: This person can't hold your attention very long. They are too busy being narcissistic about imitating the person they are around.

40. <u>Conveniently Loven</u>: Oh the love is so sweet, so new, and so fresh until the wheels start turning with how to get out of it. OOOOOh, maybe some advice from the professional manipulator who can make em do and give things in the name of "family". Yea, that's right, the pre-planted seeds of

discouragement that continues to grow in the spirit due to lack of strength and foresight. When to become a man or not because my flaws and flawed "friends" have blinded me and I just can't see.

41. Look–A-Old: This individual looks older that his former partner who is only a month older. Matter of fact, the look-a-old appears many years older than his month older former partner. I'm talking about OLDER! Whew! His sneaking around is showing and glowing. What a prize!

42. Lewebb: This syndrome drills years of hatred into young minds to be sure and stunt not only their growth, impairing their ability to see clearly. It will be years and years if these tainted hearts ever find freedom from the many years of tapes stored in their minds. Doubts, fears, and sadness stems from Lewebb.

43. Stuck–a-time: This person caused a tiff in another lifetime of years ago and continues to live in the past as if it's the present. Resentment, hatred, and bitterness flourishes for this one. Not only does this syndrome rot inside but makes it a lifetime hobby.

44. I-take-you-give-a: You have something I want then I take. You leave possession in my car, you need, and I keep. OH, it must have disappeared. You should not leave anything of value around this person; it'll be as though it never existed. WAIT! I need something, so I take and you give.

45. Pick-a-what-I-want: You and your friend go to the store to pick up a few items for dinner. A guest comes along for the ride while her spouse and yours wait at home. The guest believes you to have an endless amount of money, picks up what she wants and puts it in the shopping cart because that what she and her spouse would like to have. The clincher is, you have limited amount of money and you don't get reimbursed. That's what you get for having the right personality.

46. Expensive of most order: This particular couple goes when and where ever they can with you. You pick up the tab. Okay; it is good to share, but all the time? All the time? Well, okay. Now let's order the more expensive item on the menu since someone else is picking up the tab. Doesn't matter, they deserve whatever they can get out of you. After all, you have their friendship, what more should you want. You have more so you should feel obligated to give more, and more, and more, and more, and more and more, and . . . get the picture?

47. Fog-a-lot: My how soon this one forgets and forgets! You are out of your mind to think I said that or this or something, but I didn't say that, this, or something! You must have made that one up or maybe you're wacky or something, but you know I wouldn't say that.

48. You do but snake no do: Sounds like this one may be a new hairdo. No, sadly, it is a misguided thought that the

dangerous snake is involved. And, in truth it may be. You will be asked to do something since the snake would be way too good to do it. Think a minute. Hum. The snake will not get any urge to help in any way, but you, now you go in there like a good little person and do what a snake won't do . . . something good for someone else. But, let's reward the snake, okay now? Good!

49. <u>No, not an option</u>: Not allowed to feel bad or say no, which is in part, mental abuse. Be alert to this one.

50. <u>Maybe-jane</u>: Coulda, woulda, shoulda and maybe later. You know the type; let's do lunch daling . . . agh, it never happens!

51. <u>False-Hope:</u> To the normal person, it sounds silly. To the abuser, it is truly sincere and absolutely hopes to get your inheritance . . . idiot. Why give you hope to live when the False-Hope Syndrome is giving you strength to pick out that coffin? So studly, so low life, so badly misinformed.

52. <u>Drankem:</u> Can put away the booze and never seem to abuse. The loss is long term pickling. The toss away is permanent.

53. <u>Lac-a-dough:</u> This one is having guests over for dinner. Asks you to go to shopping for a few extra items. It'll give you a few dollars to buy all the stash. It causes a rash, every time not enough cash.

54. <u>Piglyn:</u> Showy hog in mind and spirit. Shares like a log, have fog in the brain, and never refrain from telling you how great they are all the time, all the way and every day.

55. <u>Drop-A-Lot:</u> Ah, come on; listen to the sweet sound of freezer finds and freezer drops. Open up the freezer door and BAM! BAM! And BAM! Brings back those show stopping memories.

56. <u>Look a Round:</u> Did you drop something? Well then, get someone to seek and search for you.

57. <u>Make-fu-sun:</u> The person with the magic touch. Has the self-made license to make fun of anything and anyone. The fun one is ready to run with judgments, thoughts, and screams.

58. <u>Gunlots:</u> Fun-ny! Sits at the stoplight, gunning his engine, waiting for the light to change so their car can . . . beat yours? Well, blow me down; I cannot put on a frown. This is just too funny for this clown.

59. <u>Pig-a-lot:</u> Greedy, needy, inconsiderate, and yea, greedy.

60. Interuptitis: No harm intended although harm received. No harm sent to impede. But often harm is done you see and interrupts the fun to be.

61. Pushyitis: No harm from this farm, just so there's no alarm, it comes naturally without a gate, must tell you before too late. Forgets so quickly and final too. One must cut in before the thought cuts out.

62. Natural-Bo-Bat: This person is a natural at whatever is attempted. Why good gracious why ever isn't it blimpted.

63. Menabu: In countries here and there and everywhere, very little merit is given to mental abuse. Why you might ask? Because my dear, "that's the way it is". Is it moral or right? No? The abuser can get away with it.

64. Friendly helper: Have a friend that can help you with that. It's not my ideas or theirs, but surely just because it's your idea, you must need some help in makin' it right, cause after all, it's your creativity and your ideas. Someone else is surely needed to make it clearly successful. No harm from this farm, just lack of confidence in the creative one that can only succeed if some else doesn't step in and bring it to fruition. Bring it on.

65. <u>Southern and Likin' it:</u> You are from the South, I Kaaan hear by your accent. Those people are so niiice. You feel like you are in a bowl of syrup oozing all down your chin when you are around "them". Aren't they so precious and sweet in their little mountain cabins burning wood and digging coal! Ah-hum, Whew! Them thar Northerners may be the misinformed ones who have no idea what they are talking about . . . why are so many of "them" moving South. I have family in one of those fancy Northern states and my goodness gracious, some of the nicest folk you'll ever meet and greet. As for us Southerners, well, honey, butter just doesn't melt fast enough in our art galleries, theatres, operas, world renowned research centers and more. You must be misinformed of our heritage and ability to be nice, polite, and downright hospitable. As for the coal diggin', those Northern folk sure do like their electricity.

66. <u>Turn about face</u>: This one speaks what's on the mind. No matter the season, place or time. Whether right or wrong, doesn't matter - as long as - it's the owner's chatter. Space and reason is not the point, it's what can be said in this joint. So, just go along and make no waves. It'll soon be your turn to hit the paves. Hum, do I dare or do I share? Hum, doesn't matter, you're not cut out for that kind of chatter.

67. <u>Lizzzz-zah so grand</u>: Why I am as sweet as American Apple Pie. Not only am I friendly, I will smooze so as not to lose. I will say whatever any day in any way. It doesn't matter whether it's right or wrong, just as long as my sanctimonious mind stays pea size. The prize is mine – it's mine, I say. Lands sake, I am a fake. Don't have to tell you – as - it's all see through. I'll do whatever I need to do . . . the prize belongs to me at any cost. Just ignore the frosty frost.

68. <u>Geribear</u>: Goofy in looks and actions. Thinks like a smoothie in traction. Says what is necessary to get the dough. When work

time comes, oh, what flow? Ignore requests just do it my way and always say it's information from a professional, hey. But, what kind of professional you might inquire? Oh, doesn't matter. With Clatter the fatter as a guide, it can be thrown on any side. Over and under doesn't matter . . . as long as Chatter the fatter is in charge.

69. <u>Right on –Rright over- and Right by</u>: This is applicable to anyone who has a yard that is accessible. I can park, walk or ride over your property without hesitation. I owe you no explanation. Why, it's my right to walk on, ride over and go right by without even a "hi".

70. <u>Knock on early</u>: Totally inconsiderate and bangs on your door about 7 AM. [You're fast asleep by the way] He plows up a spot in your yard for flowers and demands payment beyond reason. Then after paying this rude and crude, you go to inspect to see the spot is not only terribly small – it's not at all what it is supposed to be. Lumpy and bumpy, be rest assured this piece of "working" low life won't set foot on my land again.

71. <u>Lack facts</u>: A different way of thinking. It was a privilege although not seen at the time. You were taught to think, save, and be a land owner and money loaner of character and ethics. Many thought you came along the path with money just by the way you spoke, the way you charged forward and the way you thought. These less fortunate ones thought there were no tough times in building – it was as though it all came easy. No price was paid that the outsider could see. After all, it was clearly there and lots of it in their minds eyes. Very seldom is there no price to pay . . . and if you didn't pay it personally, believe me there is a price of hard work and sacrifice. You may not see the scenes of sweat and tears, but it's there. The individuals who cannot see are in for a long hard wait for it to fall out of the sky into their laps of ignorance. It does evolve from experience that

many will not be able to discover. This explains slow money and rich minds.

72. <u>Fast easy luck</u>: When a person is fortunate enough to earn some big bucks and have no character, yea, they can build material things. But that's the point, they build things. As we all know, things can disappear. It is the character of a man that takes a life time to build and is to be protected at all times. Character is much better than things. Do we need things, money and the survival necessities? Sure, but remember that the character of a man lives on because things do not have a heart.

73. <u>I'm The Perfect One:</u> Okay, oxymoron. There was only one Perfect One in this go around, and they crucified Him.

74. <u>Me Keepa for You:</u> This is really a nice and considerate person. Too bad she didn't realize the box that came in the mail was for her instead of a friend. It only took about four months for it to hit her over the head. OOPS!

75. <u>Momida:</u> Oh do I know it all. If I could patent crossed eyes and find some grey matter to add to my brain, then maybe I wouldn't be so intelligently glued to dumb! Yea, and don't forget I am better than you too; and well you know, better; better than – well – just somehow better – I hope!

76. <u>Unawareness Disease; One through Something:</u>

A] Can't see what you see

B] Take what I can find even though it's less than the best

C] Pride myself to be smart, but can't seem to hit the mark

D] Receive the negative that is dished out and ask for more

E] Give no credit to self-talents

F] Surely "they" are smarter – they said so

G] Learn that it's your fault even when it isn't

I] Be quiet when someone is speaking, what they say is

more important than what could possibly come out of

your mouth

J] Don't listen to your heart – listen to what I say

K] Must check everything you do – to make sure you're not

being crazy or is it just that lazy streak painted in the

middle

L] Not as good looking as someone else – if you believe

your friend

M] No Hope-No Way - is a favorite – especially if money is

Involved – goodness sakes – he deserves it more than

You

N] Give credit where credit is due – NOT! Give it all away

O] Appreciating the beautiful in nature – it isn't worth a lot.

Others are supposed to declare what is beautiful, not

You – someone else must know, but not you.

P] Being too trusting is a benign tumor that can turn

cancerous in a jiffy if the spiffy one sees your trust as

ignorance

Q] Is it becoming a sin to be too nice or hospitable or just

you? The lack of Intel for necessary scouting could be a

problem.   It's that Southern thang once again.

77.   Speecupp: Take a look around and tell me what you see. Sparkling clean and nicely painted walls – pretty marble counters – handsome furniture collected through the years – oh, and don't forget these beautiful Persian rugs throughout the modest well-kept home. Your guest comes in with a chaw-toe –backy original only one time used spit cup. Ah, the sound of grunting, hacking and spiting chaw-toe-backy while cooking fresh food to serve. It's so appealing and chillin' to the tasteful courtesy buds.

78.   New Friend knothead-Not: Walk right in, sit it right down and all at once start talking about what boobys you have – doesn't ever_ one? [No, not every one – ever one – the ever freakin' disgusting one who thinks she's so pretty and ever one must see it, whether you like it or not! So there you go pilgrim. Like it or not – this one is a goose on the loose!]

79. Oh, Okay, I'll Let you Pay: Means well – well intended – well, good company, and well fed. Thanks!

80. Doing Part: I'm doing my part. You may not see it, but I am. Partly because I don't want you to see and yes, I'm doing my part . . . you know the part that you don't see. Partly because I've done my part too many times, now, it's your turn to do my part. Partner, thank you so much and by the way, are the paychecks ready? I need my money. Heh, heh, heh!

81. Behind the Glass Barker: You've seen those small type dogs   that bark and bark and bark and bark behind those glass doors and windows? Well, with all that barking – you just know without a doubt they have clout! They will bite the ever livin' tar out of your ankle if they get loose. Yea, I call 'em the barkers – because I taught 'em and well, they bite better than me, but I'm learning!

82. Screamer: As you and I both know – there are all kinds of screamers! You know what I'm talking about . . . The one described here and right now is the one that screams and yells with each possible breath and then some! Yells, yells, and yells! Screams and screams and screams! It's hard being around the Screamer. Hurts my ears – not too good for my spirit either.

83. Calmer: No matter the situation, no matter the plan – this grand one is calm. No matter the charge and no matter how

bland, this one is calm . . . Calm as a cucumber and green as a bean. This one is blinkingly calm and clean.

84. <u>Nervous as a tick-token</u>: I'll not hyper – just excited – oh I don't know what I'm excited about – just excited I guess. I'm not hyper, just excited. I am not repeating myself! I'm just excited.

85. <u>Sash Smiler</u>: Prancing and a dancing – that's me – prancing cause I'm sooooo prêt-ty and oh how I like to smile. [Those aren't real! Can somebody please find out where she got those teeth?]

86. <u>Past Pretty to Pretty Ugly</u>: Sounds like you're asking somebody to pass the mashed potatoes. Maybe it's the turkey or cranberry sauce. Either way, it's just plain past.

87. <u>Full Mouth Talker</u>: So appealing, so delightful – so disgusting! Emily wrote those books for a reason. She even passed it down the family tree because she felt it to be important in the manners world of courtesy, kindness, and tasteful eating.

88. <u>Ig-no-rah-mous</u>: Really now! Everyone knows what ignorant means. It's the ones who can't see theirs – whether in one or many situations –that takes everyone's cake. Related to Ug-A-Lee and doesn't even know it. Sad in a way. Yea, funny isn't it. Oh, I did share that there are many types of funny

didn't I? Well there are. It's still funny. Almost as funny as watching the sleeping kitty fall off the fish tank.[No, it didn't get hurt, just got up and shook it off. We humans should try that sometime.]

89. Smilin' Major: Wanna see a dog smile? Just go away for several weeks and return to a smile so big – you could not believe it unless it happened to you – well it did.

90. The idiot sperm donor: Directed his son in the right direction for all the wrong reasons. The mother directed him in the same direction for all the right reasons. The sperm donor felt he could follow in his less than smart uncle's footsteps and be taken care of for fear he couldn't make it on his own. The mother knew he could make it just fine . . . all the young people would listen to what he had to say and what a great messenger he could be for the Author of Time and Love.

91. Just try to: Insult was not intended and none taken. You can even try to insult me and still – none taken. Blows your mind doesn't it? Give this charming one a trophy for rare finds. You will rarely find confidence this cool, this witty and this generous. She's known as the world's greatest Mom by her own three and all the rest to be – all to her credit and all my salute!

92. I know how you feel: Well special one, until you experience what I've experienced, until you've seen what I have seen

and until you live as long as me – no – you don't know how I feel.

93. <u>Intelligently Soaped</u>: I am so intelligently degreed, but watch out when it's time for those soaps. I am so stuck eyed to my programs! Hum, okay, what? I knew she'd get caught running around on that sweet husband of hers. The last episode almost gave it away, but I figured it out. Those writers aren't very smart. Huh? What you'd say. Isn't that dress a bit flashy for that scene? Yea, go ahead, make some coffee. [That wasn't the question, but, okay, I'll make some coffee.]

94. <u>Trade 'Em Cody</u>: Trade up Trade out and Trade on.

95. <u>Pay the Rent</u>: You mean actually pay the rent? You mean I'm behind? Why should I pay the rent? Oh, it's yours – well, can you explain to me why you think I plan to pay the rent?

96. <u>Moving on Up</u>: It may be okay for the Jefferson's to move up to the east side. You might want to check it out in your city before you pack those boxes. You might be moving into the blizzard of Hades if you don't do your homework and check out the area first. It may seem too good to be true – and – in some circumstances, it is. So before you commit to the lease, check with the police. Make sure to get first base and still be safe!

97. Joblose: This one is for the married lovers not married to each other. Started threatening before thinking. You go and get yourself fired – you smart thang you. Now don't go blaming someone else for your stupidity! It's just plain stupid – stupid is as stupid does.

98. Corporate Ladder: Tried this and it didn't work for me. The corporate ones thought I was the ladder. Oh, that one is too true and painful. Broken foot for helping & out the door ah flew!

99. Due to Lack of Interest: Due to lack of interest – today has been cancelled. I'm just too tired and have no interest.

100. Ride that bike: Bit by bit, little by little, and step by step. Each ounce of the way – sixteen of 'em that is – a pound down and only a hundred to go. Sure is easier to put it on than take it off. Who ever talked me into this fat girl gig was out of their ever loving thinking cap. Oh, excuse me, I apologize. Didn't mean to accuse you. I just didn't recognize that chub in the mirror!

Take a break

There is more to come.

Meantime, here are some

Ideas to think about

To

Give you more clout!

Intermission Time!

It's always a good time to stop and reassess where you are and where you want to go. Okay, the first hundred syndromes don't cover all the bits and pieces of personality that flows throughout our society or any society for that matter.

There is always going to be something we left out of the equation. [I have a mouse in my pocket George W. B. used to respond with when someone asked him a stupid question] Remember what Oliver said: no, not the "more sirs" one, but the one who stated that the only thing new is the history we don't know.

Mysteries – personalities – and more mysteries can be found as we dig and uncover the top layer. Then, once again, dig some more and find some more. As the story of mankind goes – don't try to reinvent it – it's already been done. All we need to do is discover, learn, read, watch, and keep on learning. Don't start pointing that finger at me when there's plenty of dust where you are. Remember – doing the same thing over and over and over and over expecting a different outcome each time doesn't send any salute to Albert. If you're not leading yourself, the scenery isn't going to change.

Finding happiness is not that difficult. Choosing it - is. There are lots of books to recommend, but it wouldn't do you any favors. You have to be hungry enough to read for yourself - - - all the facts going on all over this space age, spaced up and spaced out world of ours.

We have been given a lot. Doesn't have to be material – but you can turn that gift into something material that might feed you and someone else along the way. All the seeds have been scattered. Some of the seeds fell on the sand, some on the rocks, and some by the river. Not all of us will be monetarily rich, but we can find some goodness in our circumstances to be more comfortable. Now keep in mind that with this personality gig we're talking about now – the definition of what each individual calls or refers to as comfortable. Some may feel rich and comfortable to have a hot meal. Someone else may feel rich and comfortable with a fine fancy home. It's all in the eyes of the beholder and where we are in our journey. Each one of us is in a different stage of circumstances. Some are similar, but all are different. Some are good and some are not so good.

Allow yourself to be grateful and thankful. However, don't allow yourself to be taken for granted. The earlier, the better and the better, the smarter lifestyle will afford you the luxury of discovering the wonderful person that was created years ago. You were not created to be stupid, dormant, or incapable. Look around at the

different ones who may not have what you do.

The ones you may feel sorry for may actually feel sorry for you. The

ones you feel sorry for may be using much more of their lesser gift

than you do of your greater gift. Hum? Ever wonder how a young

vibrant person who swims like a swan ends up with only a voice, mind,

and spirit who goes forward full steam, and ends up as an artist,

singer, radio talk show host and more? Did she choose to lose the

se of her limbs? Maybe not – but she did choose to use what she had

with a vigor that gives hope to the more fortunate physically inclined.

She chose to be, to give, and to live full steam ahead. Don't waste

your time feeling sorry for someone you perceive as less fortunate. In

reality, they may be feeling sorry for you – not because you have

more, but because you use less of whom you are. Want to be a star?

Shine on before you can shine up and shine out.

As a storm rolls in with a boom, just remember; a time and a

season for everything. The season for me is discovery and feeling

happy to share. Really – excited like I described earlier. Excited as I

share with you about discovery and choosing my happiness is using a

gift of gab that may lift someone up and out of the drab and dark

places. And I have to remember that I can only offer the hand of care but you need to offer the hand of want to be the best you were created to be in this life, in this time and in the rhyme or reason of where we find ourselves to be in this place called now.

   So, if you choose, march forward and discover that wonderful creature you are. Go forth in much desire to use your one gift or as many as you choose to discover. It's a choice. Stay right here – right now – right on and do nothing. Or, it's your privilege to go forth in growth, discovery, and richness of character and reach out to lift someone else up that is reaching for a lifting hand. As the advertisement stated many times, it's not a hand out – it's a helping hand.

Now once again,

A Personality Syndrome II

A Personality Syndrome II

101. <u>There's a Honey and the Bees Don't Know It:</u> I like to strut and show my stuff . . . unfortunate for me there is no one around to see. Even when I strut, my, what a strut, and I do have a strut. This is one honey of a bee with no one to see.

102. <u>Buy 'Em and Sell 'Em:</u> Buy this one for what he is worth. Sell him for what he thinks he's worth. Now there is some money to be made on this one!

103. <u>If you can live with them</u>: I can live by them.

104. <u>Big grocery Bill:</u> Can't say that I enjoy a huge grocery bill each time I go shopping for food. But I do recall someone saying that it's better to have a big grocery bill any day than going to the doctor. Right G.W.B.? [i.e. a grand man of great foresight for 83 plus years]

105. <u>Foresight of it all:</u> It's better to see it as it is than to see it as you wished it were. Anyone with the gift of foresight will tell you that it's much easier to deal with something you know is coming rather than waiting for the unknown.

106. <u>Mold It – Mill It – Dew It:</u> You preach and preach and preach. If "they" could ever learn to be as good as you. Oh, you want to

rent my moldy mildewed extra house? Sure! Got a good deal for you that you can't refuse!

107. <u>Toast to Real Friend:</u> Here's to you dear friend. You talk behind my back, gas your car, drink my liquor, eat my food and borrow my money. Gosh, you're so special. Oh wait! Here's a spitting container for you while I go get you something.

108. <u>Four A.M. Blaster:</u> Radio blasting at four in the early morning and awakes house guest. Oh, you didn't notice? Oh, you just don't care. Boy! Bogie to that music!

109. <u>Take him, I keep goodies:</u> Husband brings girlfriend home to see wife. Wife doesn't blink. You can take him – I'll keep everything else [It was A LOT AND LOTS OF] – the girlfriend decided to leave since she couldn't have the goodies. Oops!

110. <u>The Good Housekeeper:</u> It was a great short marriage. She kept the house, he had to leave. She's a great keeper of the house.

111. <u>Betlyvon:</u> His female business friends – whether physical or mental, they're friends of the closest kind.

112. <u>Magic Painter:</u> Agreed to paint for peanuts. The white paint scheduled for the walls turned green . . . somehow.

113. <u>I can – U can't:</u> He's so smart – must put you down in your place not to be found. Aka true love.

114. <u>You pay and She Stay:</u> Same day start pay. Then to the doll of lower-lower – you can stay for free. Love it when doll can trick me, use me and snarl with a grin. What a win!

115. <u>Sucker:</u> Tell me what will please my ear and you can take any dough that's in the show.

116. <u>Doll Forn:</u> Watch out liars! Your daughters might marry a man like him. Yea, the cover may look different, but the contents remain quite the same. Didn't bother you before – will it later?

117. <u>Kinkisser:</u> If your friends could see us now . . . they would see some real kissing cousins!

118. <u>Married Lovers not married to each other:</u> Baby, you're the best thang that's ever happened to me. Oh, wait a minute – isn't that one just preciously yummy. Hold on dahling, let me take a look at him. Oh my, dahling, aren't you glad I can pick 'em out? I just love picking and a grinning.

119. <u>Rest-o-Days:</u> Lover to lover - chasing 'round the bed – can't you see, I ain't dead. Chase you, catch you and never let you go. That's a new one of a hidey-hidey-hoe.

120. <u>Rockin' Borrowed Car:</u> Turn the key and the music is a blasting from a long and lasting with us laughing – Sneak away-steal the pay-scream the day!

121. <u>Hills Alive:</u> Sweet lovers, wine and the parkway. Something quick and the hills are alive with wine, screaming, and more screaming. Ah, such fun. Now here we go back to our own homes and drum-drum-drum. No, I mean, drab-drab-drab. Boy that was fast!

122. <u>Made for each other:</u> Ahhhhhhhhhhhh – oooooooo- gotta get rid of the spouses first – nah, come on, let's just do it and worry about it later.

123. <u>Soul Mates:</u> Precious, I tell you, just precious. Travel them thar dirt roads with dope to hope . . . oh, we are so mateful!

124. <u>Page Lister:</u> Ask someone to name three items to choose one as a gift of their liking and wah-lah! You are given three pages of what to get –you have more, therefore, you need to give more, right? Just because you have a family – you should give me plenty – R-i-g-h-t?

125. <u>Video Sounder:</u> The TV is blastin'- company walks in – so? – The TV is still a blastin'! WHAT? SAY that again – WHAT? I can't hear you.

126. <u>Buy Me:</u> He wants a business like your parents. It needs to be in the hills – They need to buy it and he'll take it. Anger fills the air, why it isn't fair! THEY WON'T BUY ME A BUSINESS! What kind of parents do you have!!!!!!!!

127. <u>The Good Spirit and The Written Word:</u> Match

128. <u>Intellect Alone:</u> Can be deceiving.

129. <u>Impress Easy:</u> Don't be easily impressed – DO YOUR RESEARCH!

130. <u>We Shall Name:</u> Their baby was given the name of a fabulously famous up-scale car made in Europe. Questioned as to the reason they would name their child after a foreign car, they replied, "It's the only way my husband will ever have one". Oh? But this one is American made!

131. <u>U Clean:</u> "Dahlin – after much thought over this, I have decided that you need to clean houses rather than teach". UGH? Found out later that it was because he didn't want people to know that his wife had a teaching degree. Stupid – stupid – stupid! Why, you might ask? Because she had one, he didn't.

132. <u>Little Blue Jazz:</u> '"Big Blue Jazz wanted to tell you that his Little Jazz is looking for you"'. The kin lover smiled and replied with an offer to little Jazz anything he wanted. This is special!

133. <u>Hands Off:</u> Almost lost it at the party when I saw you with your husband. It was so hard keeping my hands off of you. If people could only understand how in love we are.

134. <u>Wine-Cheesecake-Fireplace:</u> More – more – more! If your spouse finds out, she'll take, take, take! Oh, just give me some cake, cake, cake!

135. <u>Accuse Me:</u> Okay. Accuse me of being a PA, PI, and CPA, paralegal, mechanic, IT Expert and more. Aren't you so nice! Thank yall!

136. <u>Boomer:</u> Sitting at your desk, in your office, in your home bothering no one when all of a sudden the windows and doors start shaking! It is like shake – rattle – shake with a BOOM, BOOM, BOOM and it is non-stop! It's LOUD as well! Oh, you heard it, ugh? Well, I had to go out to my car, in my driveway and turn on my music. It wouldn't play very loud, but it was some really nice classical music. I showed them.

137. <u>Itchy One:</u> Never satisfied, never pleased – never will be.

138. <u>Snipping:</u> Yip-Yip-Yip and Yap-Yap-Yap; that's all I ever hear . . . is yipping yonder and yapping there! Flapping this and flapping that, baby, you just don't know where it's at!

139. <u>Waiting for results:</u> This can apply to an opinion. It can be a return phone call. Goodness, it can be a memory waiting to change. Results are what they're going to be . . . it's the beginning mark when a decision to go a certain way is made. Then, we know the vicinity of the results that can occur. Sometimes, you'll even know for certain. Sometimes you can't. But one thing for sure . . . there will be results of the decision made.

140. <u>Ah, I've reached . . .:</u> Wait just a minute, partner. According to what or where you have reached will determined the definition of this action.

141. <u>Yo-yo:</u> You know that yo-yo diet I've been riding on the past few years? Well, in my humble opinion, it's a lot of fun! You don't lose any weight, but that yo-yo sure is fun to play with when you're trying to keep food out of your hands.

142. <u>Spend Mega-Mega:</u> These newly rich and famous certainly know how to spend some big bucks! I'm talking B-I-G ones! Did anyone bother to let them know that a rainy day might come upon them without even a notice?

History has been known to repeat itself. Sure is good to know your history – for non-repeats in the future.

143. <u>Line Hangers:</u> This was an observation one evening. Upon walking into the neighborhood store on the corner, I noticed a line of men standing and waiting for a turn to pay for their treasures. Each face had a smile of contentment and patience. Then I looked at the register. There she was, treating each customer like a million dollars, not rushing anyone, taking their money with a smile and to each a sweet thank you. It was like watching a line of puppies waiting for a pat on the head. What a great young lady. Somebody tell her boss she needs a raise! It's obvious that she's worth it.

144. <u>Lexie Text</u>: Not a thing wrong with this one. Just a great big thank you from GrandmaMA. GrandmaMA received a picture and text today of the cutest little two year old sitting in her high chair, smiling, with a daddy bow on her head, and a plate of yummy veggies and fruit awaiting her pleasure. What a memory and what a special dad to not only feed well, but play well. Well, I certainly hope so; He's my son, isn't he? Gotta smile on this one. It's too cute! My salute and appreciation.

145. <u>Making a Difference Day</u>: It sounds good on paper. Be careful who is making the difference, and what they are making the difference for and for whom!

146. <u>Get Me to the Bank on time:</u> This idea is simple. To receive the simple interest, gotta get to the bank on time. The idea of

having enough money to cover the checks written, get me to the bank on time!

147. <u>Slow Motion</u>: It's been one of those days when everything is in sloooooow motion. The day starts off slow when you can't seem to go to sleep the night before and feel sleepy when it's time to get up. Then, when you think you just about have it together, the day is gone. Maybe this one should be named something but I'm just too tired.

148. <u>Got to have a nap</u>: My schedule has been arranged so that I can get my gym workout today. Only problem is, I need a nap before I go so I have enough energy to go.

149. <u>Different or Really Stand Out</u>: Have you ever noticed how some people stare when they see someone that is different. One example is the young kid in the body cast walking down the sidewalk. That's not so bad, that cast came off a year later. What is sad is the little girl or boy who has a disease that makes them permanently different and onlookers stare.

150. <u>Lose fat or ugly:</u> Yes. It's true. I can lose the fat a lot quicker than you can lose the ugly. There, I've said it.

151. <u>Imagine</u>: Just imagine - if only once in a lifetime we were a group of people that became what we were created to

be . . . now keep in mind, the word imagine is part of imagination.

152. <u>Then, Okeedokee:</u> It is pretty tough to imagine a whole society at peace with themselves, much less as a group. Ever wonder what it would be like if we could become individuals that were able to unleash the ability to love, use our talents, patience, forgiveness, and foresightavailable to each life?

153. <u>Symphony of Stars:</u> Shine as if you could pass out some hopes. The task doesn't take anything from you, just something of you that reflects a flicker for someone to catch.

154. <u>Slip Away:</u> There may be a song pertaining to this thought. In this case, its meaning is different. There's a party going on, in your honor. You get tired, slip away, and go to bed. When your guests begin to leave and look for you to say good night, you're nowhere to be found.

155. <u>Intellectually Speaking:</u> Don't think so – you must have misspoken . . . there is nothing intellectual about you.

156. <u>Pull Front Yell:</u> Here you are, driving with civility, keeping a safe distance from the car in front of you. ALL OF A SUDDEN, this jerk whips in front of you with no signal of any notice. You might find yourself squeaking a little discomfort of surprise of the unpleasant nature.

157. <u>Lotion Potion:</u> You'd think that with all the products available on the open market, there wouldn't be any dry flakey skin to be found . . . ugh, think again.

158. <u>Just Too Friendly:</u> It has been observed that when someone is too friendly, there is a group of individuals who mistake this for ignorance. In some cases it is . . . to share a friendly smile or thought of encouragement to someone who is smug in their own intellectuality is not too smart if you find genuine kindness repulsive. And, some people do - really.

159. <u>The Good Child:</u> The widowed elderly mother has to go to a retirement home because of health reasons. She has been a good parent and grandparent. Her home is sold to pay for this expense. The children go through her home to pick out anything of worth and sell the house with the remnants of her life inside. Oh, and by the way, there are a few notes stuck on some of the valuables to save for the family. They just didn't have the time to take it with them. Oh, and would you store it for them until they can find the time to pick it up or find a buyer?

160. <u>The Onion A peel</u>: If they knew better, they would do better. Like an onion, layer by layer, consequence by consequence and so it goes.

161. <u>The Back Away:</u> You're at a social engagement involving mutual family. The sanctimonious one looks up, sees you and walks in the other direction. Can't say I blame her. If I had lied like she did with what and whom she is supposed to be, I would turn and run too.

162. <u>Blind and Liking it:</u> Have you ever noticed or observed someone who is clueless? It's scary. On some of the late night shows, people have been interviewed on the street. Simple history questions dumbfound them. Yea, it's scary. Our history is changing daily due to lack of knowledge.

163. <u>Mine is, Yours isn't:</u> I must tell you all about . . . oh, have you heard my . . . let me show you my . . . I am going to . . . oh, just face it, the I's have it. It's all about me anyway.

164. <u>Ohhh, say can you:</u> Oh, say, can you do me a favor? Why you are going to the store, would you pick me up something? If you're going by that place, would you stop and get me that? Oh, pay you back, what for? Don't you have plenty of money? Well, if you feel that way, I just won't ask you to do it again. Oh my – could it be possible that it would happen?

165. <u>Let's stop and have lunch:</u> You don't mind driving do you? Hey, let's stop for lunch. I like to order a lot, especially fried, deep fried and more fried. You're just ordering a salad? Why that's not enough to feed a kitty cat. Oh, can you spot me a few extra dollars; don't have enough to pay for my plenty.

166. <u>Hot water Hottie:</u> The local and famous politician, like other national figures, found that his legal troubles weren't over. Spending public money for self-entertainment is not ethical nor is it legal. Poor darling. If his baby's momma sues him, he will find another unsuspecting female to lure into his love nest. That smile is so endearing to . . . I can't think of anyone at the moment, but maybe it'll come to me later or not.

167. <u>Silly Bike:</u> The substantial woman was so dismayed . . . she made it to the gym on time. When she went to push the button to start the bicycle, for her fifteen minute ride, it wouldn't light! Help! It won't start! Oh, I understand, I need to pedal first and then it comes on . . . that's a novel idea.

168. <u>Makes A Good Friend</u>: Sitting there talking with a very nice lady and telling her how nice her husband is . . . you know just like a brother. He is such a good friend to my brother. "Well, I'm glad

he's a good friend to someone", she deliberately replied. I feel her pain — no more to be said.

169. <u>Ah, Free Sitter</u>: Ask a college student to look after your young children. Don't pay them for a week or two. And, by all means, don't give her any money to buy or provide food or entertainment for the day. Just because the mother is single, and can't pay broke you then, well, what the heck. The kids are nice, but there still isn't any money coming into the "kiddy-bank".

170. <u>Here, Take another Hunk</u>: The State and Federal Revenue took over half your money from a divorce settlement. Then, two surgeries later to the next tax period; they want an extra hunk of money cause you were in the hospital too much and too late. Isn't that special?

171. <u>Need Face Fix</u>: Would the state please collect extra taxes from me so the governor can get her face lift. Besides, my jalopy and surgeries don't compare to those needs!

172. <u>Smile Robber</u>: The smile can outshine the Wilshire Cat and the warmth ooze smoother than pancake syrup. Watch out! You'll get robbed of your trust, spirit, and yes, the pocketbook as well. After all, she needs it — you have it — why not let her take it! She knows how to take it — with the experience she has, hey, you won't know what hit you till it's too late! Don't feel too bad . . . you're not the first and you certainly won't be the last! One of the smoothest robbers you'll ever experience!

173. <u>Ignorance at a Glance</u>: This one is so ignorant! How ignorant you might inquire? She's so ignorant, you can't see through the glasses on her nose. She's so ignorant; she doesn't know how to define courtesy much less use it. She's so ignorant; she doesn't even know how to speak her own language correctly – ugh? Vowels and consonants are agreed? She's so ignorant; she doesn't know that vowels are different from consonants because a vowel can have two to three sounds – not just one! Don't frown – that was supposed to be the major in her master's degree!

174. <u>Too Long:</u> Ignorance at a Glance was so ignorant; she took up too much space so this definition is short!

175. <u>You Answer – Me not</u>: Just because I call and you don't answer – don't get upset with me when you call and I don't answer. Funny isn't it? It can go both ways.

176. <u>Like words – Like Music:</u> As stated in the Intermission Time –   different people see different meanings from the same words. Same is true for music. I may enjoy classical and you might enjoy blues or jazz. You see something I don't see in the sound and I see something – well, you get the picture. That's just it! Paintings offer the same variation of interpretations. Ah, isn't art great and fun . . . so much to give and such little space to absorb?

177. <u>Made in the U.S.A.</u>: Have you ever noticed that it is now made in China? Have you ever noticed that the sun is getting brighter or are we just becoming thicker? Are the abilities to use our talents becoming so intellectual that we are selling out to a power willing to take ours? That's not too bright! Maybe the powers that have decided this are too willing to sell us out for personal gain . . . theirs! In the long run – it will bring us all down unless we claim our land back and start to work again – the old fashioned way.

178. <u>The Collection</u>: Don't be more willing than me to sell my work – the demand isn't there when you're too willing to sell out too cheap . . . the collection isn't there if someone else comes along and "makes" it happen. The accomplishment will be when the products sell by request. Just remember – you make it and they will come . . . you push it and they will run.

179. <u>Teachers</u>: Ah, the reward. I've seen the good and I've seen the bad. There's always the reward – whether good or bad – it is what we teach from our actions that can cause reactions. It is what we show that brings a tow or the glow.

180. <u>All Over Again</u>: This has been stated different ways with the same meaning. Different covers – same guts. Different words can make it the same all over again; whether you realize or not.

181. <u>Treasure Scraps</u>: You see scraps than can become treasures. Someone else sees scraps as useless pieces of junk to be burned

and trashed. Some scraps are trash, but it takes the keen discerning eye to know the difference.

182. <u>Insane, Brilliant, Nutty or All of the Above</u>: Times of talent or times of tell – either way – it just might sell. Give it a try or make it dry. Only the effort will show the signs and then I can say – it's all mine!

183. <u>The Surprise Visitor</u>: Oh what a nice surprise! Just wish you could have seen me when it was a smaller size!

184. <u>Wanting To Share</u>: Is it really the desire to share or is it the need for someone to care? A puzzle is not meant to confuse you see, it just wants to be whole and meant to be.

185. <u>Get Out and Run</u>: For some, this is the only way to have fun. For me, crank on the engine, turn on the air and off I go with a nice cool flair!

186. <u>My Best is Yet to Be</u>: As we improve over time – just remember, without reason or rhyme, the best is yet to be - for all we do and all we see, it gets better with each and every try. There is no way for another day except to improve – improve – improve!

187. <u>Guess the Price</u>: If we could put a price on all we do – it could turn into a mark-down for all we say! If we are careful from day to day – it can still be tricky along the way. Either is the choice and either is the prize. Whether we arrive first or last – depends on if we choose the fries!

188. <u>Speaking Terms</u>: It's been a while since we last spoke. A relationship put on hold is no joke. Time heals they say for a brighter day. The point to make is to know – that time waits for no man - to finish the show. The sooner the mend – the quicker to pen up the hurt and get rid of the dirt. The time is now without delay - it's always possible not to have another day. Time to play and time to love. Time to work and time to find. Time to know when it's time – time to give and time to heal. It's time and it's now.

189. <u>The Pool</u>: The memories I give are not a bit more important than the memories I receive. The others can see and I appreciate that. But more important is that on this journey I go; the contentment is in this knowing that the love is not how pretty I am [and I am] but in the sweetness of the moment is this heart that overflows in the cart. Full of fragrance and full of care. You need not worry about the fare. All is free and paid for you see. All I need to be is the ole oak tree.

190. <u>The Butterfly</u>: The worm all wrapped up and yucky hanging there. How can one expect to see much care? Until one day – as if by surprise, it opens up and fills the eyes! The wings how pretty in showy disguise. How wonderful to offer and what a pretty offer it is. To find the beauty there all along. Just

depends upon the song. Sing high or low – doesn't matter you see. It takes all kinds to make a symphony. The music was soothing and snuggly to boot. The result is there - for the world of care.

191. <u>Hurry Up! It's Late</u>: This one is simple as simple can be. You hurry and you hurry then its wait, wait, wait. I don't understand why and maybe you can tell – the reason one has to be in a hurry. The waiting is painful for this entire flurry. So, if you please, just hurry, hurry, quickly! I need to wait through all the prickly little pieces and sit until it ceases.

192. <u>The Information</u>: You must be aware of the penalty stare. There are pages and pages of writing to do. The writing and writing and writing and more . . . just then, someone walks through the door. They call your name – mistake it not. It's time to show your plot. Now if the information is not up to date – it will surely affect your fate!

193. <u>Pain Relief</u>: New medications advertised on TV have possible side effect of death. Sounds like some people you've heard of that make you feel good and have the pleasure of stabbing for the kill.

194. <u>Sharry Sue</u>: There are some you can freely share and then there are those who will allow you to share with them. And again, you can share with them. They have

nothing to do for you. Just remember this Sue – she'll
not ever share with you.

195. <u>Sad Bride</u>: Young and undeveloped foresight, she is excited
with delight. Just learned that her betrothed sells drugs. She
smiles and shrugs. I love the good with the bad. It is terribly
sad attaching to this cad. When little ones come along, and
they will, what fate lies ahead can be foresaid. The tragedy
awaits these innocent gaits. It is not new, but ole so blue. To
know that lives will hurt this bad. If only someone to share –
the light that could prevent all this despair.

196. <u>So Excited</u>: I could spend and spend and spend to supply lots of
surprises to show my love how much I care! It doesn't matter
that it takes a lot of batter! The love is deep and oh so steep. It
does not always supply enough you see – so I use all that I find
to be – for in this short span of space we have – I want us to
enjoy each flower of fragrance so fab!

197. <u>Surprise Treasures</u>: Knowing how you love the new found
treasure, it is a delight to see you smile with pleasure. One
more and then I find another for you. So wrapping it up is the
only thing to do!

198. <u>Hanging Head</u>: Pleasures found in the dirty round can only
make the heart forsake. For in sneaking Asti in rounds of play –
there is always a price to pay. The squealing, the music, the
mates on hold can only bring discomfort untold. It shows in the
face the awful disgrace – your place of distinction has fallen.

Down under they go and below the flow – never to be a
number one – you know.

199. <u>Not Extraordinary</u>: They feel supreme. They find delight.
Touching and holding through the night. So different are
they so happy with prey. They burn the bridges so none
can follow. It's sad for them. Blind with whom they
wallow. The trick is to find the way back home.
Unfortunately for some – they must succumb. The
bridges they   burned – would not bring return. So there
they are – ordinary in every way, the same ole – same
ole day to day.

200. <u>Think Afore</u>: Before you do and before you say. Think
about results that cause dismay. Immediate release
could threaten police. It's not worth the effort you see.
For in the end – we need to find peace. So often others
are left in the dirt, didn't mean too, just felt right for me.
Didn't think about the hurt – it just felt right – don't you
see?

Break Time!

You've seen the good and the bad.

It could be happy or it could be sad.

Open up those hearts of care

It will help to pay the long hard fare.

The ideas shall continue next time!

Epilogues to Be

Now you know. History repeats itself. Each generation will strive to improve. Others before have gone through this door. The technology expands with talent and clout. The human factor claims no doubt that with each experience there is some gout.

Before you speak and before you act, be sure to know more than part of the fact. Time so quickly goes through space – just take a quick look at my face. The youth it was is no more. I gave it a shot that in the end was not so hot. You never know when waiting for the ship you find yourself at the airport. So, laugh at this silly and be sure to reach – into the books that can teach. Learn all that you can and more if you please. It will give upper than this tease. Arm yourself rich with knowledge. More is better if more can grow. More is better if more can show. There is more to give and more to have – riches of happiness contended and glad.

Character is more and honesty is great. Look and learn when determining such hate. And know in your heart – it's never too late.

Reach for quality in building your fate. Strife will always find a way onto your path. Just be ready to give it your wrath. Stay clean as can – so you will see. Life can produce satisfaction galore. Through each and every door today – be your best in every way.

A Recap of the Journey for your convenience

Years ago, a musical artist wrote a song and implied that if we don't stand for something, we could fall for anything. This was true then and now. The people of talents have improved as each generation comes into view. History is rich in character for sure. We have made so many improvements from the days of old. Unfortunately, knowing what we stand for may not be the solid foundation in which we were built.

New and improved is wonderful if it means nurturing to have a foundation that stands upon roots of deep. We can face devastating storms of many varieties when we have strength to hold us solid. Confusion is plenty and full of despair. When we know what is good and act upon it, then our foundation remains unmovable. When we know and don't act – it can take away the nourishment needed to keep the roots strong.

When the time comes that we no longer see or feel the need for a foundation that's solid, the ground can move in ease with the wind.

Just look around at how much better to have all the fun and more entertaining things to fill our days with this ton of stuff. Things will change when humans do. Character and ethics change for better or worse when humans do. Over once again – we roll the dice and need to grow. It's good to see and be in the know. Sorry to say – it doesn't always show. What is good and lasting is not always easy nor does it taste more than queasy. Immediate satisfaction has become the highlight of the day. Delayed gratification will pay much more than ever imagined – in most cases.

The route to go will be yours to show. If it doesn't always end up the way you thought, you can know it was yours – left uncaught.

Put This on for Fit

1. <u>Un-Ruden to:</u> When a pseudo smiling pro comes your way to say words of hurt today – the Un-Ruder – in a most sincere way, smiles and declines to be rude back in anyway.

2. <u>Kind of the Different:</u> This receiver stands in wonderment when the giver shouts words of condescending. The hurt came through the soft she knew. There is work ahead to make this shed.

3. <u>To-Others time:</u> No matter where we go, someone always recognizes the glow. There is always time to say hello!

4. <u>Small in Size:</u> The little ones always know and try to show. A smile and a hug to let her feel – to see her brings happy thoughts because she cared in spite of their faults.

5. <u>Howdy Sweetheart:</u> She invited the friend who tried to let her pay for her celebration today. She smiled with sincere reply and let them know kindly with a sigh, she had no dough to float their flow.

6. <u>Waiting and Smiling:</u> All patiently lined up down the row, for they had no other place to go. They waited patiently to pay and see that smile of thank you darling would tide until next they come appareling.

7. <u>Excited Birthday Surprise:</u> You vowed your love with a diamond – yet to be sealed with a band. You criticize my finances yet give plenty away to your friends. I spent too much for your birthday surprise and can't wait to see your eyes. Instead I get a reprimand for giving my heart today. I'll pay my bills - thank you - and smile away the gills.

8. <u>Doing without:</u> There are those who must have the best of all – as I recall. I, on the other hand, may have to do without – but you can be rest assured that there is no doubt - of my clout. The ones who see the dollar sign are not at all like me. I use the green and try to stay on a beam that shines the light. After all, as I take flight, there is no other that has my sight.

9. <u>Over Talker:</u> When trying to share fun and loving words and get cut in the middle. I have no choice than to close my voice and choose to keep the chiddle. No repeats for me – no repeats for you – I'll stay on the diddle and keep my chiddle. And the cow jumped over which moon?

10. <u>They Paid Cash:</u> It's so sweet of you and easy to notice. Their orders were oh, again, full of nutrition and booze. You must have provided the cash so they didn't feel the ooze. They paid so freely before heading out the door. It was so obvious that you really paid . . . a free meal to celebrate is so nice you

see – as long as you pick up the tab – they'll be – right there to nab.

11. Isn't She Thoughtful: Even though there is no faith in what you do, she'll gently hint a few. Here are some ideas that may meet your need. The minds are so very young – it won't matter how you can't teach. It'll all come out in the wash when you reach. Now isn't that sweet?

12. Let Me Do: Let me do this for you – there is no way you can see. I'll pat you on the head and steer you clear out of fear . . . I do mean well.

13. Let's look over the shoulder: She's smart and bright and very polite. She can't possibly do what I think she should. I'll look over her shoulder for she can't handle that boulder. Of course I didn't know she was the one that created it! She can't be that smart – I still need to look over her shoulder and protect her from that boulder.

14. We disowned her years ago: Not knowing how much would change – we have all we need – the fornicating one outsmarted her he thinks indeed. As years go by – we begin to see her fly. Maybe we can claim her once again – after all she hasn't any friend. The money hasn't anything to do with it – we have all we need. Of course if she wants to share the greed, we'll make her feel better to patch this plead.

15. <u>Here we go again:</u> So many before have walked through that door. That for sure you can depend. What is this? Someone different you see? Oh my! Hope he will keep this catch indeed – for there is not much to feed. The heart is there and oh so fair! She is the keeper he searched for so long. Just hope the wait didn't alter his gait – she is a beautiful song. Some will try to make her fly, but the suitor is smarter I trust and will bring her in to a banded zone called home.

16. <u>Natural Roses:</u> We went to see the final home of theirs. Flowers of white and pink that she put on their stone that shone all along. The care she brings along with all the things that a daughter can do. I love you dad and I love you mom. I will stop by again to say my hellos. You go with me to the farther ways but it's always here I come to bring – fresh flowers to your stone each spring.

17. <u>Tall and Bright:</u> She's grown so tall and smart I see. So little, so sweet and now in a tweet – she's grown. A neighbor maybe, my heart is hers; a daughter so precious I would love to have claimed. She's smart and grown and precious still. A family now she had to show – so sweet and smart like she is - aglow.

18. <u>Other:</u> It's true he likes to enjoy the spoils of his work everywhere. Whether here or there – he brings home the gold – some others he will always hold. His family so near – so dear to his heart. The medals are great,

but his family, his mate, is by far the sweetest medal a
man can make!

19.   Getting Ready: It's exciting to see the little faces this year. They
      come through my door just ready to explore with no fear! My
      hands are full and hearts to be filled with each new face - Lord
      give me the grace to help each one – to prepare the knowledge of
      their age – and send them later to a greater stage.

20.   Of Age: Of age they may be but inexperienced you know. They
      show their oats but sometimes miss the boats. The age takes
      more than just young minds of time – its sage that makes the
      blend comprehend sublime.

BRIGEOR

Born and raised in North Carolina, armed with a heart full of care,

BriGeor enjoys making learning fun. Studies and experience have proven that

the more fun you have learning, the more you can learn. And, the more you

learn, the more you can learn!

BriGeor and Major like to ride because it is easier and more fun

with the windows down!

More information on BriGeor next time!

A BriGeor Collection

www.ingramcontent.com/pod-product-compliance
Lightning Source LLC
Chambersburg PA
CBHW060207290526
45789CB00003B/1191